# WORKPLACE SPIRITUALITY AND LEADERSHIP

KAILASH KUMAR SAHU

ISBN 978-93-5458-108-3
© KAILASH KUMAR SAHU 2021
Published in India 2021 by Pencil

*A brand of*
One Point Six Technologies Pvt. Ltd.
123, Building J2, Shram Seva Premises,
Wadala Truck Terminal, Wadala (E)
Mumbai 400037, Maharashtra, INDIA
**E** connect@thepencilapp.com
**W** www.thepencilapp.com



DISCLAIMER: *The opinions expressed in this book are those of the authors and do not purport to reflect the views of the Publisher.*

# Author biography

Kailash Kumar Sahu is pursuing Ph.D. in Management and currently Guest Lecturer in Management at Pandit Sundarlal Sharma (Open) University Chhattisgarh. He has published 5 research papers and 2 self-learning materials (SLMs). His research interest areas are human resource management, consumer behaviour, and leadership.

# CONTENTS

# INTRODUCTION

Workplace spirituality is itself an important ingredient in creating effective leadership, satisfaction among employees, and overall organisational performance. It also helps in reducing stress, conflict, absenteeism and employee turnover. In 21st century, it becomes very important to retain your competent and talented employees in the organisation for the long term for sustainable growth. There are researches available in the knowledge domain which explain its importance in improving leadership, resulted in higher satisfaction and overall organisational performance. Thus, it becomes important to understand workplace spirituality and its effect on leadership.

# LITERATURE BASED ON WORKPLACE SPIRITUALITY

**Beazley (1997)** conducted research to develop the spirituality assessment scale by measuring each dimension in the organisational setting. The author concluded that spirituality contains faith relationship with a transcendent power as being independent in the material world. The relation with transcendent and non-material elements and engagement to something which is greater than self is depicted in the term "spirituality".

**Freshman (1999)** utilised grounded theory to develop definitions based on various applications of workplace spirituality and played a significant role in defining this phenomenon in his own study. The author revealed the findings:

1. "Not anyone, two or even three things can explain about workplace spirituality; this includes the whole universe for an explanation."

2. "There is no universally accepted answer to the question, 'What is workplace spirituality?'"

3. "Definitions and applications of workplace spirituality are a unique and different person to person. Therefore, when planning to incorporate

or implement spirituality in the workplace or any group, again the objective should be deriving definitions from participants themselves."

4. "There are many possible ways to understand workplace spirituality as being a complex and diverse area."

**Wheatley (1999)** pointed out to self-creating and self-organising system in nature with an objective for organisations to work more effectively by accepting the natural cycle of change, stability and renewal. Thus, the "spiritual" or continuously renewing nature of these processes has been interpreted as a significant design for constructing workplace spirituality.

**Ashmos and Duchon (2000)** identified that the world of corporate work is changing. The research was focused to investigate some objectives, namely; Where Americans work? How they are involved in work? specifically, since the beginning of computer technology emerged as offering effective communication, creating isolation and a sense of disconnection with work among employees at the workplace who are engaged in communicating with other employees through computers? Following points were noted with regard to spirituality at work among the American workforce:

1. The American workplace has become a place where employees are often discouraged due to reengineering, downsizing and layoffs that happened in the past decade.

2. Due to the decline of churches, extended families, neighborhoods, and civic groups, the workplaces are considered a major source of creating community so as to feel connected with others.

3. Philosophies from Zen Buddhism and Confucianism facilitate stress values and meditation such as finding loyalty to one's group and spiritual center in any activity and interest about Eastern philosophies and Pacific Rim cultures.

4. Global organisational leaders are forced to incorporate the employees' creativity at work for creating a competitive cutting edge.

5. There is a growing understanding with regard to life' meaning and purpose because of knowing the fact about life's biggest uncertainty – death.

**Krishna Kumar and Neck (2002)** conducted research to review the distinct perspective of workplace spirituality, discuss the various benefits of implementing at the workplace and investigate the different ways of incorporating the spiritual-based culture at the workplace. Authors argued that a different perspective of spirituality is a positive thing for the organisation if the manager strives to understand distinct views of spirituality and encourages them among the employees within the organisation. The authors highlighted that those organisations, who are involved in motivating and helping employees or willing to offer "individual encouragement" in order to achieve spirituality, directly increase organisational performance.
**Wong and Psych (2003)** stated that "To be effective,

spirituality is required to integrate into the corporate culture by demonstrating into the organisational policies and practices on the daily basis". By supporting the other outcomes, organisations wanted to take the fullest benefits of spirituality with regard to morale and productivity which leads to the complete organisational transformation. When it happens, the following effects can be seen in the organisation:

1. Management learns to listen honestly and prepare a safe place where employees can put their opinion forward without any fear of consequences.

2. Management will build an environment for sense of community and encourage the feeling of sense of belongingness after breaking down the different levels of hierarchy.

3. Willingness to reflect the importance of the meaning of life and moral implications in order to take significant decisions.

4. A shared attitude is reflected that the products and services will be beneficial to the community and humanity.

5. Management will give importance to employees on the basis of 'who they are and 'what they can become' as compared to 'what they can do for the company'.

6. Management and supervisors will treat employees in a respectful, responsible and caring way because

employees are any instrument to be used and exploited.

7. Management will strive to find a solution to resolve conflict in a spiritual way rather than issuing an ultimatum or firing employees reluctantly.

8. There will be a change from autocratic leadership to participative servant leadership, which encourages empowering, delegation, and cooperation to employees.

9. The improvement will be seen in morale, loyalty, job satisfaction and productivity.

10. The organisation will gradually become meaning-based as well as purpose-driven.

11. Management with a mission will replace management of efficiency and control.

12. There will be the change that can be observed from a fear-based environment to a love and support-based environment.

13. Management practice and decisions will be directly based on spiritual values such as integrity, love, kindness, hope, honesty, respect, and nurturing.

14. The spiritual dimension will be completely incorporated with work-life such as relationships, planning, organising, budgeting, negotiations, compensation, etc.

**Brown (2003)** conducted empirical research to discuss the potential of spirituality, specifically the positive and negative sides of spirituality at the workplace. The author concluded with a positive side by saying that spirituality can offer guidance, wholeness, and connectedness to the organisation. On the negative side, the author said spirituality is in trend (with sinister suggestion) which, when uncovered, is expected to be short-lived and ineffective. Though, there are not much researches backing up which result is more expected to happen.

**Hicks (2003)** analysed linkages between religion and the variables i.e., pluralism, spirituality, and leadership in the workplace. This research also focuses to identify the relation between religion and spirituality in the different workplaces. The outcomes indicated workplace spirituality is considered as an alternative to religion or more than religion itself in the different workplaces. The researcher also recommended that spirituality in the workplace includes adherence to a certain kind of thinking about self, work, and organisation.

**Ashar and Maher (2004)** conducted research to study the concept of success with mid-and senior-level executives in a federal government agency. The authors aimed to define success from their perspective based on materialistic elements such as money, power of position, and status symbol. They were expected to create connection, balance, and wholeness of these elements to describe and define success. But, as opposed to the expectation, the participants associated the concept of success with spirituality by stating that to become successful one needs to embrace spirituality as well. This research revealed that spirituality and the notion of success are linked. The authors also proposed a conceptual model of success consisting of four elements of both success and spirituality.

**Gull and Doh (2004)** conducted research to review, integrate and expand the existing research on workplace spirituality. The research recognises a huge cost incurring to businesses due to the absence of spirituality in the workplace and thus, offering "transmutation" to the workplace, established based on spiritual values. The researchers argued that spirituality can be the basis of ethical conduct at the workplace. Incorporating spirituality in the workplace makes the environment more soothing and creates a moral obligation among employees to behave ethically in the organisation. The authors have discussed the relationship between individual spirituality and ethical conduct in the workplace and predicting Aristotelian virtue play mediating role between these. They argued that spirituality creates general values in individuals based on four elements, namely; interconnectedness, self-transcendence, one's ultimate concern, and meaning and purpose. These elements guide individuals' actions and behaviour. Practicing these spiritual values over time becomes virtues that significantly and positively lead to benefitting the organisation.

**Kinjerski and Skrypnek (2004)** conducted exploratory research to create a better understanding and defining spirit at work. 14 professionals as samples for the study were chosen who have not only experienced spirit at work but also involved in researching or encouraging spirit at work. Based on the participants' explanations, the study found that spirit at work is a different state that has affective, cognitive, spiritual, physical, interpersonal and mystical dimensions. This state involves physiological stimulation, positive influence, one's belief that his work makes a contribution, a sense of connection with something larger than self, sense of engagement with something meaningful for the community, a sense of connection with others, and a sense of perfection and transcendence. The importance and usefulness of a comprehensive definition of spirit at work for theory advancement, research, and practice are discussed.

**Marques, Dhiman and King (2005)** researched to develop an integrated model and a comprehensive definition of workplace spirituality for enhanced research in this field by future researchers and also to develop a mechanism for the industry for creating a spiritual mindset in the workplace. The authors found some crucial elements in the study which are as follows:

1. Spirituality in the workplace lies in the belief in oneself and his/her positive outcomes, even in the hard times.

2. Workplace spirituality gets encouraged among the employees in the organisation when people receive good care in terms of physical, mental and spiritual.

3. It begins with the acknowledgment that every entity, individual or group, has a spirit.

4. It does not only turn into good results within an individual's work environment, but ultimately in an improved and performing workplace which leads to a better society at large.

5. Spirituality is not religion, but rather a connection with one's deepest inner life. Workplace spirituality, therefore, has no connection in the enforcement of religion at workplace.

6. Interconnectedness was found the basis of workplace spirituality. This factor is significant in the creation of an environment in the organisation where every employee is encouraged to engage with each other.

7. Workplace spirituality is not an ethereal phenomenon, and surely it does not negatively affect business performances. In contrast, implementing spirituality in the workplace does encourage innovativeness and creativity within the employees, which further results in enhanced productivity and better overall performances of the organisation.

8. The applications of workplace spirituality can be applied for the future global developments. Since it has been observed that government and non-profit organisation are not able handle issues such as climate change, health care, security issues and many others, this transfers the responsibility into the hand of private sectors. Now it becomes significant that business settings should bring deliverance into all these areas by applying more empathetic approach in their performances, and this empathetic approach comes with people factor. The author suggests that if the employees are treated well in terms of that they truly matter

for the organisation, then the employees get encouraged to increase their productivity and put utmost effort in increasing the organisation's position as in the national, global and regional level. Once these changes are done in the workplace which nurture the spiritual mindset of employees is established, the improvement in the societies can be seen where these organisation exists.

**Fornaciari, Sherlock, Ritchie and Dean (2005)** reviewed 29 empirical studies which developed 65 new scales during 1994-2004 in the area of spirituality, religion and work (SRW). Based on the Hinkin's (1995) methodology for assessing questionnaire scale development as a model, authors reviewed: (i) inductive vs. deductive approaches in item generation issues; (ii) sampling and reliability/validity assessment in scale development issues; (iii) convergent validity testing in scale evaluation issues. The study found that majority of the researches (86%) had shown item development process for developing new scales; deductive approach was used as primary method for item establishment i.e., based on the existing literatures. In the process of scale development, nearly 45% of the researches used factor analysis for assessing the constructs; and in that, less than 25% had described information related to factor retention criteria, such as eigen values. About internal consistency, only 45% of studies had shown the values of coefficient alpha. However, in some articles, scale establishment process related information was described quite detailed and reflected statistical rigor. Nearly 38% of studies had shown any information with regard to scale validation. Similar conclusion to Hinkin (1995), authors found that scale development practices in the area of spirituality, religion and work (SRW) to be inconsistent.

**Kinjerski and Skrypnek (2006)** attempted to develop and validate the Spirit at Work Scale (SAWS) with the help of 333 employee participants (occupation ranging technical, clerical, administrative, academic, and maintenance) working in a large mid-western university. Earlier participants were asked to respond to 102-item instrument. Factor analysis predicted four distinct factors: sense of community, mystical experience, engaging work, and spiritual connection. After factor and item analyses, final 18 items were finalized to establish a new scale. The analyses showed no relationship between new spirit at work scale (SAWS) and gender, income, age, or education. However, SAWS scores were significantly correlated with marital status and occupation. Management and professional staff have shown higher level of spirit at work as compare to technical, administrative, clerical, or trades staff. Employees who are widowed, divorced, or separated have predicted higher spirit at work as compare to those workers who are single/unmarried. Authors concluded about the new scale and this research by putting significant points at the end; (i) the study will help to create enhanced understanding of the construct; (ii) direct future researchers to validate the new scale (SAWS); (iii) this will help to examine the individual and organisation outcomes related to spirit at work; (iv) help in testing the effectiveness of different programs to enhance spirituality in the workplace; and finally, (v) provide practical application in the organisation.

**Rhodes (2006)** has found six effects that can be correlated with the model of workplace spirituality. The six effects are:

1.  Enforcing Sustainability

2.  Contributing Values

3.  Cultivates Addition

4.  Building Principles

5.  Prizes Creativity

6.  Encouraging Vocation

At last, author concluded that these above six elements help in designing a partial framework for implying spirituality in the workplace and impacts in the Western business culture. To retrieve and recognize the spiritual nature of people and the significance of implementing the "complete person" in the workplace will continuously be transforming the business processes within the United States.

**Badrinarayan (2008)** conducted research to review and compare two concepts to workplace spirituality facilitation. The author uses two real life descriptions to draw workplace spirituality facilitation. The study also compared between the two adopted approaches in terms of features and benefits and provided implications for future research and practices. The author found that the first approach is more focused to facilitate the transmission of organisational values and processes which can be identified as an organisation-centered approach. And, the second approach is mainly emphasised to transform or develop spirituality among individual employees in the organisation.

**Edwards, Van Laar, Easton and Kinman (2009)** conducted research to develop measurement scale for work-related quality of life to capture perceptions of working environment and employees' responses to them. The authors were mainly focused to explore the factor structure of the work-related quality of life scale for higher education employees. Primary data were collected of 2136 employees from four higher education institutions in the United Kingdom. Levels of work-related quality of life scale for each factor were found consistent with the previous studies related to academic employees. However, higher education employees, in the analysis, were found dissatisfied with their jobs and careers, dissatisfied with working conditions and control at work and were reported that they are stressed out at work. Results evidenced that work-related quality of life scale proves itself as a psychometric instrument in both aspect i.e., multidimensional and uni-dimensional level in order to assess the quality of working life of higher education employees.

**Petchsawang and Duchon (2009)** researched to develop the measurement scale of workplace spirituality at Thai company which is engaged in food and bakery deliveries. Due to its well managed and efficient reputation, they got 3800+ employees to participate in this research. The authors began with five-factor (i.e., connection, compassion, meaningful work, mindfulness and transcendence) definitions of workplace spirituality aimed to helpful in developing measures for workplace spirituality by conducing investigation into the psychometric properties of the measure. Two points were in focus in this analysis i.e., first, workplace spirituality is multi-dimensional, and second, each dimension or component has a connection with other dimensions and cannot be seen in isolation. The confirmatory factor analysis was applied and the five-factor model was reduced to four-factor model i.e., compassion, meaningful work, mindfulness and transcendence. The revised scale seemed important in terms of measuring spirituality in an Asian, Buddhist-centric workplace. Because the scale was inspired from conceptualisation of spirituality in Western (i.e., Northern American) work context, it may have utility in a Western work context.

**Cash and Gray (2010)** conducted review study to investigate the current state of religious and spiritual activities in the organisations and also to discuss the influence of employment law on such practices. The authors provided a comprehensive discussion and interpretation of religious and spiritual practices incorporated in the business organisations. This study found the degree to which the countries like Pakistan army and teaching were confronting religiosity and spirituality in the workplace. Participants were selected from different age groups, gender and working positions and, then, the case study technique was incorporated. The outcome revealed that both areas (i.e., Pakistan army and teaching) experienced religiosity and spirituality at the workplace to a certain level but, on the other hand, was unsuccessful to discover any organisation where the workplace spirituality is truly implemented.

**Griffiths (2010)** researched to examine the spiritual values (SV) and coaching in the workplace with the perspective of coaches by incorporating the interpretative phenomenological approach (IPA). The analysis revealed the significance of spiritual values of coach and the features linked with spiritual values which are required in the global economy, multi-cultural and for the reliance and longevity of an organisation. The author added that the true values and passions are the essential elements in the coaching approach, especially when 'aiming the higher order'. In the end, a 'Spiritual Helix Coaching Model' was presented for providing a potential direction to coaches working within the context of spiritual values (SV) development.

**Khasawneh, Alrjoub and Zawahreh (2010)** researched to establish and validate a psychometric questionnaire of spirituality in the workplace (SWQ) with the help of 1008 faculty members working at six different universities of Jordon. After analysis, five factors were found concrete with all 22 items of questionnaire. The outcome revealed that workplace spirituality is multidimensional construct and can be used to measure by different variables. The authors suggested that university administrators and HR professionals in higher educational institutions should identify the notion of spirituality in the workplace.

**Liu and Robertson (2011)** researched to propose new theoretical conceptualisation of spirituality for the development of new spirituality scale. The authors used 2,230 individuals to test and cross-validate the spirituality scale using structural equation modeling. The authors found the construct of spirituality consisting three distinct factors i.e., interconnection with human beings, interconnection with a higher power and interconnection with nature and all living beings.

**Sheng and Chen (2012)** conducted research to examine

the causal relationship of workplace spirituality with varying perspective of Chinese workers. The outcomes revealed that the causal relationship of workplace spirituality is a continuous movement based on the views of Chinese workers. Beginning from the understanding the environment, an individual would introspect and increase the workplace spirituality practices which would directly influences their self-emotions, interpersonal relations and also the external environment. Finally, the change of surroundings would reversibly impact the individual's way of perceiving environment.

**Lips-Wiersma and Wright (2012)** researched to develop and validate a comprehensive measurement scale of meaningful work with a sample of 167 participants employed in the different organisations of New Zealand. Result indicated that the scale is multidimensional and process-oriented measurement tool which covers varying complexities of the construct. Various dimensions like unity with others, expressing full potential, developing inner self, being vs. doing, self vs. others, and serving others were included in this comprehensive scale. They added that it also helps in measuring the inspiration and its connection with existential need to be real and grounded.

**Pardasani, Sharma and Bindlish (2014)** attempted to investigate the Indian spiritual traditions that how it facilitates spirituality in the workplace. The findings suggested an integrated framework which explains that doctrine of Karma Yoga, Guna Theory, Pandha Kosha, tradition of Loksangrah, and Daivi Sampat model can provide assistance in facilitating the workplace spirituality dimensions (i.e., meaningful work, interconnectedness, transcendence of self, alignment with organisational values, and holistic growth and development).

**Ahangaran, Khooshebast and Vahedi (2016)** attempted to investigate the effect of spirituality in the workplace through Meta-analysis using available scholarly literatures. Authors also focused their study to develop a comprehensive model of spirituality. The outcomes of the meta-analysis indicated that spirituality encourage organisational citizenship behaviour which further influences on individuals' creativity and innovation. The enhanced employee commitment, leadership success, and entrepreneurial behaviour are also affected by the presence of spirituality in the organisation. Authors presented a comprehensive model at the end as a result of thorough literature review.

**Ahmed, Arshad, Mahmood and Akhtar (2016)** described the importance of human spiritual dimension to build an effective human resource development (HRD). Authors suggest that spiritual intelligence is missing link which needs to be identified in order to develop morally qualified human resources. Additionally, authors also discussed the emerging interests in spiritual intelligence and its implications for human resource development (HRD). The article indicates that in order to achieve higher standard performances of employees, spiritual development of individuals should also be considered along with logic (IQ) and emotions (EQ). The authors concluded, hence, in order to develop holistic mechanism in human resource development, the emerging notion of human spiritual quotient and its different dimensions must be covered.

**Shrestha (2016)** researched to further validate and develop a measurement scale for workplace spirituality in an Eastern context as the four-dimension model of workplace spirituality consisting 22 items was earlier developed and validated by Petchsawang and Duchon (2009) with taken sample from Eastern Buddhist-centric culture for capturing workplace spirituality in an Eastern context, specifically Nepal. The results supported the four-dimension model (i.e., meaningful work, compassion, transcendence and mindfulness) of the workplace spirituality scale. The results of confirmatory factor analysis and reliability analysis revealed that the workplace spirituality scale developed in Thai context is generalisable to Nepali context and all four dimensions are neatly reproduced in this context. Other statistical analyses indicated significant convergent and discriminant validity of the scale.

**Jain (2016)**reviewed existing literatures and attempted to develop a model for workplace spirituality aiming to provide a better performing and sustainable organisation. This model contains three dimensions, namely, transcendence via work, practice of virtue centric code of conduct, and sustainability perspective. At the end, the authors suggested that this model offers different techniques to inculcate workplace spirituality and its nourishment in the organisation.

**Pawar (2017)**researched to evaluate the nature of influence of an individual spirituality and organizational spirituality on employee's experience of community at work and meaningful work variables of workplace spirituality by examining the direct effect and moderating effect models empirically. The findings showed a significant support to the direct effects model but found no support to the moderating effect model. Within the direct effects model, organizational spirituality was found a much stronger relationship than the individual spirituality of employees with the variable of workplace spirituality (i.e., community at work and meaningful work).

**Pandey (2017)** reviewed workplace spirituality and explained its different themes, impact and future research directions. Author firstly explained the distinction between religion and spirituality based on the existing literatures. Afterwards, different themes and impact of workplace spirituality on several organisational outcomes were discussed on the basis of various empirical studies. At the end, the author concluded by explaining the significance of spirituality at the workplace and its future research directions.

**Pradhan, Jena and Soto (2017)** attempted to develop and validate a comprehensive model for the measurement of workplace spirituality with the help of 361 professionals belonging to different manufacturing and service organisations in India. Results indicated four distinct variables that develop a new model of workplace spirituality: compassion, alignment of values, spiritual orientation, and meaningful work containing 30-items.

**Neal (2018)** reviewed workplace spirituality and its role in the workplace aiming to provide a comprehensive knowledge on how workplace spirituality has significant role on different organisational outcomes. Author enumerated six major sections in this research: (i) historical background and trends, (ii) research methodologies, (iii) organisational exemplars of workplace spirituality, (iv) spiritual practices in the corporate sector, (v) outcomes research, (vi) recommendations for future research in the field of workplace spirituality.

**Bella, Quelhas, Ferraz and Bezerra (2018)** reviewed workplace spirituality as a sustainable human manageable factor with regards to organisational efforts for long term growth. The authors focused to showcase the relationship of workplace spirituality at three levels i.e., intrapersonal, interpersonal and institutional using 202 research articles. The authors found that workplace spirituality is focused in fostering opportunities for personal growth, opportunities to contribute significantly for society and being more attentive to superiors, subordinates, colleagues and clients. Spirituality in the workplace is for meeting your needs for inner life, purpose and community which provides more sustainable way to live, work and grow.

**Kasinathan and Rajee (2019)** researched to analyse the six dimensions of workplace spirituality (i.e., compassion, mindfulness, spiritual connection, sense of community, meaningful work, alignment amongst organisational and individual values) and its significance in organisational outcomes based on previous scholarly journals. The authors found that the six dimensions of workplace spirituality are the pillars to build a strong spiritual organisation with committed professionals. They added that its a model of workplace spirituality to serve as a partial framework for engaging in a broader conversation in the organisation and impact in the modern business environment.

**Rocha and Pinheiro (2020)** reviewed and attempted to comprehend the concept of organisational spirituality with the help of 61 published scholarly journals. Authors stated that there are three kinds of spirituality perspective available in the management studies i.e., individual spirituality, workplace spirituality and organisational spirituality. They also argued that spirituality can also be considered from a religious perspective. Authors found two clusters, namely, workplace spirituality and organisational spirituality. Cluster analysis was run which indicated that there is a huge possibility to research in the area of workplace spirituality and organisational spirituality. The proposed concept of organisational spirituality is an organisational identity inspired from its values, practices, and discourse which is blend of individual and workplace spirituality directed by leaders and others that is caused by organisational environment, culture and knowledge management. This spirituality creates value and social good which can be seen in the organisation's vision, mission, image, and organisational values.

Petchsawang (2020) discussed mindfulness and workplace spirituality and its relationship in the context of Thailand. Results revealed that there is a gap found in the management field which needs to strengthen by conducting qualitative research method and applying quasi-experimental design, and researching the antecedents of workplace spirituality. For practical incorporation at the workplace, mindfulness techniques such as mindful break, guided landing etc. can be used achieve enhanced mindfulness. The organisations should be more focused at encouraging the virtue, moral, and ethics among the stakeholders in order to improve workplace spirituality. Additionally, human resource management practices and organisational culture should be aligned with the spiritual values wand in this process; the leaders could play as a role model at the workplace. The sustainability of workplace spirituality can be ensured if the all the different departments of organisation could be aligned.

# LITERATURE BASED ON WORKPLACE SPIRITUALITY AND LEADERSHIP

**Joseph (2002)** conducted a case study on leaders' and spirituality in the following two phases i.e., first, a phenomenological description and analysis of recently appointed leader, the principal and chief executive of UK college; and the second is to conduct a longitudinal case study (18 months) examining the insightful changes within the college by applying interview technique on the seven staff members. The researcher compared between the principal's management style and interpersonal approaches adopted by the principal as experienced by others. The underlying processes refer to demonstrate the effect of a strong leader and the probable connection between leadership, power and spirituality. The findings predicted that spirituality is a highly subjective concept with a unified definition – it is argued after creating best understanding from a phenomenological – perspective; it indicates that there is a significant difference between US and UK regarding the awareness of spirituality among staff within organisations; the literature is excessively positive regarding the consequences of spirituality-inspired leadership; a leader's spiritual motivation, not easily observed by others, can be a positive and significant influence for the organisation as well as for an individual; proximity is essential for a leader; explicit showcase of spiritual motivation is likely to provoke significant reaction which may be negative sometimes; leaders who are strongly motivated due to spiritual beliefs are tend to put strength from beyond themselves. The influence of spiritual motivation performs as an additional aspect of being competent leader which can be easily operationalised or quantified. It is potentially of insightful significance to the individual leader, facing consequences in the outside by relating the personal manifestation.

**Fry (2003)**, based on intrinsic motivation model, developed a causal theory of spiritual leadership which helps to implement vision, theories of workplace spirituality, hope/faith, spiritual survival and altruistic love among the employees. The author also examined the religious and value-and-ethics-based leadership theories and found that, to create motivation among employees, leaders must be following their core values and communicate them to their employees through various actions and vision to develop spiritual survival sense through calling and membership. Further, the author argued spiritual leadership is not only one engaged in motivating individuals through leadership theories, but there are many other motivation-based leadership theories which are conceptually distinct, less conceptually confounded and parsimonious. And, by implementing calling and membership as the two predicting needs for spiritual survival, spiritual leadership theory can be called as the comprehensive of religious and value-and-ethics-based leadership approaches.

**Reave (2005)**reviewed over 150 studies to investigate the consistency between spiritual values and practices and leadership effectiveness. The author found the consistency between spiritual values and practices and leadership effectiveness which eventually leads to motivate employees, creating positive ethical environment, encouraging positive work relations, inspiring trust and finally, accomplishing organisational objectives. Leaders' effectiveness can also be seen as increased productivity and profitability, reduced employee turnover, improved employee health and higher sustainability at the workplace. The author accounted number of outcomes with regard to the importance of studying spirituality in leadership, spirituality as a foundation of work motivation, the link between spiritual values and leadership success and spiritual practices affecting to leadership effectiveness.

**Dent, Higgins and Wharff (2005)** conducted research to analyse several academic research articles for how they characterize workplace spirituality, explore the nexus between workplace spirituality and leadership, and find out the essential factors and conditions for encouraging spiritual leadership theory at the workplace. Major focus was to find out the distinction within the eight areas in the workplace spirituality literature: i) definition, ii) connected to religion, iii) marked by epiphany, iv) teachable, v) individual development, vi) measurables, vii) profitable/ productive, and viii) nature of phenomenon. The authors coded 87 scholarly research articles into these eight areas and found that many researchers correlated spirituality and religion, and that many either have found, or hypothesize an association between spirituality and productivity. The emergent areas provide challenging new avenues in the way of developing leadership theory.

**Fernando and Jackson (2006)** researched to find out the influence of religion-based workplace spirituality on decision-making of Sri Lankan business leaders. The findings showed that religion is significantly affecting the emotional, motivational and judgmental qualities of business leaders' decision-making in Sri Lanka. In addition, the leaders' decision-making was found to be connected with transcendent and eventually being a source with solace, guidance and inspiration.

**Crossan, Vera and Nanjad (2008)** discussed transcendent leadership as a framework for the fulfillment of various responsibilities of strategic leaders in the current dynamic environment via adapting cross-level mixed effect model. They said that the transcendent leader is called as strategic leader who guides within and amongst the self-level, others and organizational-level. Self-level leadership comprises the duty of being self-aware and establishing individual strengths. Others-level leadership includes the system of interactive impact a leader has upon followers. Organizational-level leadership involves the arrangement of three interconnected fields: environment, strategy and organization. Suggestions were provided with regard to the relations between leadership and other various level and organization performance.

**Fernando and Nilakant (2008)** conducted a research to establish workplace spirituality-based self-actualisation model with the help of Sri Lankan business leaders. The primary data were collected of 13 Sri Lankan business leaders through face-to-face and in-depth interviews. The findings indicated that when business leaders confront spirituality in the workplace, they use to grow, become and evolve as self-actualised individuals. The need is primarily worked as major desire to become or connect with one self. The results showed that the self-actualising work provides a method to incorporate comprehensive workplace spirituality, but it is also found that the devoid of challenges is generally linked with religion-based workplace spirituality practices. The author suggested that this study would provide implications for research with regard to spiritual leadership and ethical decision making in any other diverse cultural setting despite of different social, cultural and geographical differences.

**Fernando, Beale and Geroy(2009)** conducted an exploratory study to find out the components of leader's spirituality and also test these components against the present discussion of spiritual leadership in general and transcendental leadership model in particular. The findings indicate that the spiritual leader's highly internal locus, a strong passion as caring nature for his followers and spirituality characterise the transcendental leadership concept.

**Vandenberghe (2011)** attempted to develop an integrative model with the help of proposed model of Fry and colleagues on spiritual leadership and envision how spiritual leaders can affect employee commitment in the workplace which further leads to enhanced job performance, retention, psychological well-being, and organisational citizenship behaviour. The model also posited sense of membership and sense of calling as mediating variables in the relations between spiritual leadership and four essential elements of commitment (normative, affective, continuance-sacrifices, and continuance-alternative). Three moderators (personal spirituality, materialism, and climate for spirituality) of spiritual leadership were introduced in this model. On the basis of recent studies related to spirituality and commitment in the workplace, authors proposed certain hypotheses which directs to further research on spiritual leadership and commitment. Author also discussed different levels of analysis and generalisability of the model as key issues which can be used in future researches.

**Freeman (2011)** discussed the concept of spirituality and its influence on the creation and effectiveness of servant leadership. The proposed model of the study assumes that spiritual beliefs (e.g., hope and faith in God) as influencer in the development of behavior and values of servant leader. Additionally, the model also postulates that spiritual practices (e.g., meditating, praying, and reading scripture) plays as moderating variable between servant leadership behavior and the outcome variable, leadership effectiveness, as perceived by followers. Hypothesized relationships among four variables (i.e., spiritual beliefs, spiritual practices, servant leadership behavior, and leadership effectiveness) were revealed and proposed testing propositions and measuring methods.

**Gibson (2011)** investigated that what factors of spirituality may influence the principals' leadership and how its further influence teachers and teaching practices. The research conducted in three public primary schools, situated in North Island of New Zealand, comprising three principals and nine teachers as respondents. Results revealed that principals believed their personal meaning of spirituality were integrated, filtered and fitted into different professional tasks, leadership styles modeling, and, subsequently, contributed to their resilience. They also believed that their spirituality was reciprocally affected by their school context. However, teachers suggested that spirituality can be more influential and positive in principals' leadership when it comes with integrity, professional competence, and quality care for others. Teachers' responses explained positive emotions and practical influences to spirituality in their principals' leadership while some teachers expressed uncertainty and a few explains incidences which resulted in some negative feelings. At the end, author concluded that integrated nature of spirituality into principals' leadership was found very much effective and contributed into the reliance of leaders which further influences the teacher and teaching in the context of school.

**Riaz (2012)** aimed to carry out an empirical research to examine the relationship of school principals' self-reported spirituality and their transformational leadership behaviours. This study also explored the connection between spirituality and transactional leadership behaviours using the theoretical framework of Bass and Avalio (1984) in order to conceptualise transformational leadership. Analysis explained that principals' spirituality is found to be connected with transformational leadership. Additionally, a multiple regression analysis indicated, with five measures of transformational leadership, that spirituality is significantly and positively associated with transformational leadership behaviours of individuals. A multiple regression with learning combination of all transactional and transformational leadership measures were found predictors of spirituality. Finally, inspirational motivation measure of transformational leadership accounts a significant amount of unique variance independent as compare to other seven measures of transactional and transformational leadership behaviour in predicting spirituality.

**Abdullah, Ismail and Mydin (2013)** examined the mediating effect of school principals' leadership behaviour between workplace spirituality and leadership effectiveness in Malaysian secondary schools. The outcomes indicated that the level of workplace spirituality practices was very high in the Malaysian secondary schools. It is also found that workplace spirituality is significantly correlated with leadership practices of school principals which directly associated with leadership effectiveness. Furthermore, leadership practices were found as mediator in the relationship between workplace spirituality and leadership effectiveness. The authors also identified that workplace spirituality leads to effective leadership practices which is directly involved in enhancing leaders' effectiveness in terms of higher performance and commitment. Hence, the authors concluded that the school management should fully utilise the role of workplace spirituality and leadership practices as a mediator with regard to increase the teachers' performance and commitment.

**Davis (2014)** researched to determine the relationship between self-transcendence and servant leader behaviors among senior leaders and their followers at New Thought Spiritual Centers in the US. The researcher concluded that there was a significant correlation between the self-transcendence and servant leadership behavior. Further, it was also found showing partial relationship between the leaders' self-assessed self-transcendence and self-assessed servant leadership behavior.

**Barney, Wicks, Scharmer and Pavlovich (2015)**

discussed about the transcendental leadership based on their previous studies and understanding on spirituality. After the thorough discussion, they concluded with saying that they need transcendental leaders who can shift from self-interested ego to collaborative and co-existing nature based on the principles of ethics and justice.

**Sukanya (2015)** carried out a correlation study examining the interrelationship between workplace spirituality, psychological well-being, leadership effectiveness, and work outcomes using a sample of 630 working professionals at different IT firms of South India. Analysis explained a significant and positive interrelationship between workplace spirituality, leadership effectiveness, psychological well-being, and work outcomes. Additionally, workplace spirituality mediates the relationship of leadership effectiveness and psychological well-being with work outcomes.

**Muhdar and Rahma (2015)** researched to examine the effect of spiritual intelligence, leadership, and organisational culture on organisational citizenship behaviour among employee of Islamic Bank in Makassar City. The outcome revealed that spiritual intelligence, leadership and organisational culture were found to be significant and positive on organisational citizenship behaviour.

**Meng (2016)** reviewed and discussed the theories of spiritual leadership at the workplace. They also discussed about modern organization related to vision, motivation and culture-driven activities in achieving the goals and objectives. In the end, the researcher stated that the 21st century showed to become the cultural driven organization by values, encourage the workplace to struggle and strongly achieve a shared vision and all this will happen with an effective and motivating leadership.

**Kumar (2017)** researched to review the spiritual leadership concept and how it influences to organizational performance. The researcher found that spiritual leadership contains elements such as vision, selfless love, faith and organizational commitment. Every organization has the capability for the growth and success and the key is effective leadership. Spiritual leaders simply pursue secular methods and experiences to achieve success but will not be capable of attaining real spiritual leadership. People pursue spiritual leaders who realize the god agenda and who recognize how to shift them onto it.

**Wahid (2017)** researched to investigate the effect of spiritual leadership and workplace spirituality on knowledge sharing behaviourof employees of telecommunication companies in Malaysia. The results revealed that there is a relation between spirituality leadership and compassion and also the relation between workplace spirituality and motivations to share knowledge. Further, they found relationship between motivation to share knowledge and knowledge sharing behaviour, between spiritual leadership and knowledge sharing behaviour, between spiritual leadership and motivations to share knowledge, between spiritual leadership and workplace spirituality, and between workplace spirituality and compassion.

**Khari and Sinha (2017)** reviewed the influence of workplace spirituality (individual and group level) on knowledge sharing intentions by implementing decomposed planned behaviour. Authors argued that the varying perspective of workplace spirituality and its specific focus on inner spirit, sense of interconnectedness, meaningful work, and alignment with organisational values and mission positively influences the knowledge sharing attitude, perceived behavioral control, and subjective norms. Moreover, transformational leadership has also found significant in encouraging knowledge sharing.

**Sani, Wekke, Ekowati, Abbas, Idris and Ibrahim (2018)** researched to investigate the moderating role of workplace spirituality between spiritual leadership and the organizational citizenship behavior from Islamic perspective (OCBIP) of employees. With the entire 105 employees of Bank Sharia Sidoarjo as sample, the results indicated that the spiritual leadership has a positive influence on organizational citizenship behavior from Islamic perspective (OCBIP). It is also found a significant moderating effect of workplace spirituality between spiritual leadership and organizational citizenship behavior from Islamic perspective (OCBIP). Here, the place of workplace spirituality is completely moderating. They added that the good understanding of organizational citizenship behavioral concepts intensively set in mind due to this Muslim behavior is likely to demonstrate better organizational citizenship behavior. Muslim employees would believe that any decision taken not only impacts their life but also their future hereafter.

**Ali and Zaky (2018)** conducted study to examine the relationship between spiritual values and practices and leadership effectiveness. The research focused on two different perspectives i.e., first, the obscure realm of emotions and intangible ideas and the second, a practical and scientific area of inquiry. The outcomes demonstrated a positive and significant correlation between spiritual values and practices and leadership effectiveness. The author also found interactive effects of spiritual values and practices on leadership effectiveness. This research suggested that organisation should incorporate spiritual values and practices to enhance leadership effectiveness.

**Wang, Guo, Ni, Shang and Tang (2019)** conducted research to explore the effectiveness of spiritual leadership on employees' task performance, innovation behaviours, and knowledge sharing behaviours among the energy sector employees of Mainland China. Conducting multilevel analysis in order to test the proposed hypotheses of the study, the results revealed that spiritual leadership was found positively and significantly correlated with employees' task performance, innovation behaviours, and knowledge sharing behaviours, when the authors controlled the similar meaning variables like moral leadership and benevolent leadership, and ruled out alternative explanation of ethical leadership.

**Adnan, Bhatti and Farooq (2020)** focused to investigate the interrelationships between ethical leadership, workplace spirituality and employee work engagement. Authors also aimed to assess the role of workplace spirituality as mediating influencer between ethical leadership and employee work engagement in order to achieve better organisational performance. After in depth study of several literatures, authors found that the leaders are the motivational source which boosts workplace spirituality feelings among the employees through demonstrating ethical leadership behaviours, hence encouraging the better employee engagement in the organisation. Furthermore, it was also found based on the several studies that workplace spirituality mediates the relations between ethical leadership and employee work engagement in the organisation.

# LITERATURES BASED ON WORKPLACE SPIRITUALITY AND OTHER ORGANISATIONAL OUTCOMES

**McLaughlin (1998)** emphasised the connection between spirituality and profitability by saying, "a growing trend in the various organisations across country encouraging spiritual values at the workplace by indicating several examples of improved profitability and productivity. The researcher recommended that those organisations who wanted to stay competitive in the 21st century must provide a greater sense of meaning and purpose – key dimensions of spirituality, at their workplaces. The researcher pointed out that in current highly cut-throat competition, the best talent searches for the organisation which recognises their inner values and offer appropriate opportunities for individual development and community services, not just the high income. McLaughlin further enforces that the incorporation of spiritual values at the workplace as guiding principles which leads to significant positive financial effects in business.

**Nijhof, De Jong and Beukhof (1998)** have determined that "a successful organisation does not emphasis to make most of the human competencies by utilising and exploiting their employees, but to stimulate the commitment among their employees". However, Lynn Stallworth (2003) aimed to investigate workplace spirituality rather the extrinsic factors such as remuneration and benefits. The outcomes would be benefitting the Malaysian accounting organisation in promoting and implementing the correct sense of spirituality in the workplace. By recognizing the spiritual aspects which reinforces the affective commitment of employees, it would help in retaining the highly committed auditors, as considerable turnover rate in the public accounting environment in Malaysia is interpreted as the undesirable higher costs and efficiency losses such as the training and development costs of employees and recruitment and training costs for new hires.

**Burack (1999)** discussed about the newer work life and organisational culture which results an improved experience of working employees and, ultimately, reach to a sustainable growth. Author discusses about spirituality in the workplace based on different research, thoughtful analyses, also including his own experiences and observations. Terms like trust, ethics, credibility, and wisdom are the indicator of these approaches.

**Tischler, Biberman and Mckeage (2002)** thoroughly reviewed and presented several theoretical models in order to examine the possible linkages of emotional intelligence and spirituality on organisational performance. A few studies explained that emotional intelligence and spirituality are the same, but others do not, whichever the case, it has proven in almost every study that it leads to better organisational outcomes. At the end, authors concluded that it is unclear that whether emotional intelligence can be developed at the workplace, but it is clear that developing individual's spirituality is possible. Many studies showed the positive results of developing spirituality at the workplace.

**Rego and Cunha (2007)** researched to investigate the influence of five dimension of workplace spirituality (i.e., alignment with organisational values, enjoyment at work, sense of community, opportunities for inner life and sense of contribution to society) on affective, normative and continuance commitment. Sample data were collected of 361 employees from 154 organisations. Analyzing through correlation, regression and cluster technique, the author found that five dimensions of workplace spirituality showed 48%, 16% and 7% of unique variance for affective, normative and continuance commitment respectively. They also added that when people experience workplace spirituality, they feel more attached and involved in every activity of organisation, they experience a sense of loyalty/obligation towards organisation and feel less stressed and instrumentally committed.

**McGhee and Grant (2008)** discussed in their research about the relation between spirituality and ethical behaviour in the workplace by explaining the process with a model. They also discussed about the relation between religion and work. Various researchers strived to understand their work through religious lenses. Recently, a significant change has come before in relation to this. The change is that spirituality, as compared to religion, helps to understand the link between the individual and modern pluralistic workplaces. Spirituality is viewed as the positively affecting aspect to various organisational outcomes as sourced from the various socio-cultural factors. The researchers revealed that the implicit discussion is the notion which facilitates and encourages spirituality at the workplace for an enhanced ethical behaviour at the personal level and improved ethical culture/climate at the organisational level. The critical aspect to understand is that how individual spirituality converts and enforces ethical behaviour of an individual at the workplace. The entire process has been explained through a model in this research.

**Scroggins (2008)** researched to examine the antecedents and outcomes of meaningful work using a person-job fit approach. The author found that person-job fit perspective proves to be significant predictor of meaningful work. Furthermore, meaningful work has also indicated significant connection with intentions to exit the workplace. Author suggested that meaningful work was found a strong indicator as the other traditional job attitudes with employee turnover.

**Marschke, Preziosi and Harrington (2009)** researched to investigate the relation between workplace spirituality and organisational commitment. In this research, workplace spirituality and organisational commitment was considered as stand-alone factors. This research was designed to infer, develop, analyse and present the research which demonstrates the relation between spirituality in the workplace and the individual's perception in connection to the organisational commitment. The main objective of this research was to examine the factors which would further impact the growth of employee development, lowering employee turnover, improved job performance, employee retention and higher profitability as it connects to the organisational goals and strategies. This study revealed that there is an extensive belief that to survive in the 21st century in the challenges like economic recession and global competition, it is required to employ the spiritual connection among the employees. As all the evidences and research results shows that there is a relationship among the variables. The pioneering results of this study clearly indicate a positive correlation between workplace spirituality and organisational commitment which may lead to change individual and organisational lives entirely.

**Nasina and Doris (2011)** conducted a study to examine the influence of four dimensions of workplace spirituality (i.e., team's sense of community, alignment between organisational and individual values, enjoyment at work and sense of contribution to the society) on affective commitment. The researchers showed a positive contribution of workplace spirituality to affective commitment. Using a sample of 153 auditors from four big public accounting firms situated in the northern region of Malaysia. Simple random sampling was used for data collection. Applying regression analysis on the collect data, the results showed the sense of contribution to the society, team's sense of community and enjoyment at work have significant impact on the ogranisational affective commitment. The outcome helps the employers to understand the significance of the three variables of workplace spirituality (i.e., the sense of contribution to the society, team's sense of community and enjoyment at work) which motivated the employers to deploy workplace spirituality with regard to improve their employees' affective commitment. This will, eventually, increase the positive outcomes such as creativity, trust, honesty and commitment and further enhance the organisational performance and success in the long run.

**Petchsawang and Duchon (2012)** researched to examine that how an organisation can enhance more productive practices by facilitating and motivating the inner spirituality of employees at the workplace in an eastern context. The authors conducted two studies to investigate spirituality among employees to increase productivity in the organisation. First study found that those employees, who practice meditation on a regular basis, have higher workplace spirituality scores than the employees who do not practice meditation regularly. And the second study was conducted using quasi-experimental study showed that employees practices insight meditation. Further, the data did not present concrete results for the direct effect of meditation but it does reveal that spirituality has direct effect on work performance. Moreover, the research found that meditation practice is partially mediated between workplace spirituality and work performance.

**Bell, Rajendran and Theiler (2012)** conducted research to investigate the mediating impact of spirituality at workplace on well-being, ill-being and job stress amongst Australian academics using the spiritual model of stress and health. The primary data were collected of 139 academic staffs as sample working in Austrian universities using self-structured questionnaire consisting quantitative measures of spirituality at work (individual, work-unit and organisation-wide spirituality), job threat stress, job pressure stress, well-being and ill-being. Using bivariate correlation analysis, the results showed that spirituality at work, job stress, well-being and ill-being variables are correlated moderately with each other. Furthermore, using multivariate analysis, spirituality at work was not found as mediating variable between job stress and well being or ill being. But, job threat stress was significantly and positively indicated a decrease in well-being and increase in ill-being. The authors concluded that further exploration of spirituality at work will provide a better understanding regarding the potential benefits to the organisation.

**Mat, Romli, Mat and Noor (2012)** conducted research to investigate the impact of workplace spirituality dimensions (conditions for community, inner life, and meaning at work) on the effectiveness of teaching for academicians in the public university in Malaysia. Structured equation modeling was employed for the framework examination. Authors chose 4 research universities, 4 comprehensive universities, and 12 focused universities for the study, where 300 questionnaires were distributed among the lecturers. The structured framework helped in revealing the relation between endogenous and exogenous variables. Results showed that there is a significant and positive relationship found between workplace spirituality and teachers' effectiveness in Malaysian universities.

**Bhunia and Das (2012)** investigated to find out the impact of workplace spirituality on the motivations for earning management. Total three regions, i.e., northern, central and southern, were selected and 2 colleges/universities were selected for obtaining sample. Total 50 employees/workers of colleges/universities were selected as primary respondent for interview. The empirical findings evidenced that workplace spirituality is found the new insight of individuals directing and influencing their professional and personal lives. Such influences encourage the individuals on the acknowledgement of self-group relationships, and the actions of individuals. Therefore, spiritual awareness plays mediating role between organisational spirituality and earnings management. Moreover, the mediating effect is considered greater than the direct effect of organisational spirituality on the motivations of earning management. Additionally, the findings showed that there are no significant variances in the awareness of workplace spirituality among employees who have different religious beliefs. Though, a solitary confidence of individuals may not be sufficient to amend current chaotic situations with regard to earning management. Hence, earning management is essentially highly significant in the opportunistic behaviour of management.

**Sheng (2012)** researched to develop and validate the measurement tool of workplace spirituality in the view of oriental culture which investigates into varying organisational conditions. The author collected empirical evidences of 51 participants through Focus Group in Taiwan which further led to content analysis using critical incident technique (CIT) in order to examine the workplace spirituality and work analysis and its causes and effect on individuals, particularly on employee performance, on the basis of relations between work and workers. Author analysed interview data using critical incident technique (CIT) to develop the study questionnaire.

**Agbim and Oriarewo (2012)** researched to investigate the effect of spirituality dimensions (i.e., hope/faith, vision, altruistic love, membership and meaning/calling) on entrepreneurship development. The collected data were analysed using multiple regression analysis. The study showed that meaning/calling, altruistic love and vision was found significant indicators of entrepreneurship development. The authors suggested implementing these spiritual dimensions in their entrepreneurial development curriculum so that the budding entrepreneurs can be trained and become more effective.

**Heydari, Soltani, Hojati and Heydari (2013)** attempted to study the relations between spirituality at work and organisational commitment. All the working personnel at Sports and Youth offices of Khorasan, Iran (440 employees) were considered population for the study. Using stratified random sampling, 205 employees were chosen as sample on the basis of Krejcie & Morgan Table. A standard questionnaire related to spirituality at work and organisational commitment whose reliability and validity were supported by university lectures and Cronbach's alpha coefficient ($\alpha$ = 95% each). Descriptive and inferential statistics (Stepwise Regression, Pearson Correlation Coefficient, one-sample t-test, and ANOVA) were applied on the collected data. Findings indicated a positive and significant connection between spirituality at work and organisational commitment (r=0.69). 56% of commitment variance was recorded between spirituality at work, organisational and individual levels altogether.

**Sorakraikitikul and Siengthai (2014)** conducted study to investigate the role of organisational learning culture being an enabler of knowledge sharing behaviours and workplace spirituality. The study focused to examine the relation between organisational learning culture and workplace spirituality and mediating effect of knowledge sharing behaviour in this relationship. The data collection was done through convenience sampling method with the help of self administered questionnaire from 2,419 employees working in different industries, namely, banking/finance, health care, transportation, consumer goods, and hospitality in Thailand. Structural equation modeling was applied to test the proposed hypotheses of the study. The outcomes indicated a positive and significant effect between organisational learning culture and workplace spirituality. Moreover, knowledge sharing behaviour showed partially mediated the relation between organisational learning culture and workplace spirituality.

**Jena and Pradhan (2014)** researched to find out the relation between workplace spirituality and work-life balance among various employees and executives of manufacturing public sector undertakings in the Eastern Indian sub-continent. With sample of 206 employees and executives using purposive sampling, they found a moderately significant association between spiritual competences with work life balance irrespective of demographic profile. The outcomes recommended that both the variables are significant in developing an effective behavioral intervention at the workplace.

**Tagavi and Janani (2014)** researched to examine the association between workplace spirituality and organisational climate among teachers of physical education in Tabriz city. The primary data were collected of 179 physical education teachers as sample out of 344 teachers working in the state schools in Tabriz city. The teachers were selected randomly using the Morgan's table for determining sample size. Based on the analysis, the authors found a strong and positive association between workplace spirituality and organisational climate. The outcomes also showed that the all dimensions of workplace spirituality (i.e., sense of community, alignment of values and meaningful work) have a significant relationship with organisational climate.

**Paul, Dutta and Saha (2015)** researched to investigate the effect of workplace spirituality on work-life balance of women executives in IT sector companies in India. With sample of 308-350 women executives, they reported that the work-family conflict has been affected the decreased employee satisfaction, increased job stress and intention to leave, and lower individual performance in the organization. In addition, they also found that high job demand, high job involvements and lack of career opportunities were some aspects of dissatisfaction which directly lead to work-family conflict that causes, eventually, negative work-life balance among women executives in IT companies.

**Agarwal and Lenka (2015)** reviewed on the work-life balance of women entrepreneurs. With the help of selected researched papers, they stated that working-women executives undergo through various problems with regard to work-life balance. Family responsibilities and related roles create a problem of role conflict. For solving this issue, they are required to create balance between work and personal life style. To develop flexibility and control in their personal and professional life style, they need to start their own business. By doing this, they will engage in innovation, job creation and economic development with their entrepreneurial abilities.

**Mousa and Alas (2016)** conducted research to find out the linkage between workplace spirituality dimensions (i.e., meaningful work, sense of community and organisational values) and organisational commitment approaches (i.e., affective, continuance and normative) among the public primary teachers in Menoufia, Egypt. The public primary teachers were observed showing low level of organisational commitment at work. The authors distributed 200 questionnaires to the participants and received 150 questionnaires for the analysis. The findings showed that sense of community and meaningful work had a strong and positive association with organisational commitment approaches (i.e., affective, continuance and normative), while organisational values had very weak relationship with the organisational commitment approaches among the public primary teachers in Egypt.

**Singh and Chopra (2016)** studied the interrelationship among workplace spirituality, work engagement and grit. A sample of 275 full-time employees from Delhi NCR was finalised for the study using convenient sampling. Correlation analysis was applied for examining relations between workplace spirituality, work engagement and grit and ANOVA was used for testing the influence of demographic variables (i.e., age, educational qualification, and tenure) on workplace spirituality, work engagement and grit. Correlation results found a significant and positive association between meaning at work and work engagement (r = 0.359, p<0.05) and ANOVA results revealed that educational qualification, age, and tenure was found significantly differed across variables i.e., work engagement, workplace spirituality, and grit.

**Alas and Mousa (2016)** researched a qualitative case study at Menoufia province (Egypt) to examine the relationship between organisational culture variables (i.e., involvement, mission, consistency, adaptability, and knowledge sharing) and workplace spirituality dimensions (i.e., sense of community, organisational values, and meaningful work). Authors distributed 120 set of questionnaires using stratified random sampling and returned 100 filled questionnaires from teachers working in public schools at Menoufia province (Egypt). Correlation and regression analysis were applied on the collected data and findings revealed that it was false to assume that all variables of organisational culture have a significant relation with workplace spirituality dimensions.

Charoenarpornwattana (2016) researched to investigate the workplace spirituality practices in the organization, to study the human resources practices and to study the various benefits of workplace spirituality in the organization. The researcher picked 28 employees from "Company A" for the interview-based research. Based on the analysis, the researcher found three major themes i.e., "workplace spirituality practices", "workplace spirituality benefits" and "human resource practices". The researcher concluded that the findings of this study include a significant contribution to our knowledge base related to the utilization of workplace spirituality and human resource practices in the organizations of Thailand.

Chinomona (2017) researched to explore the quality of work-life, perception of work and expectations towards work on the commitment of employees' long-term career in the Gauteng province of South Africa. With a sample of 250 managerial and non-managerial employees, the results demonstrated that there is a positive correlation of quality of work life, perception of work and expectations towards work on the commitment to employees' long-term career.

**Vyas-Doorgapersad (2017)** explored two hypotheses in this study that, (i) workplace spirituality improves the employee wellness and has positive influence on improved productivity; and (ii) workplace spirituality affects male and female employees differently (gendered perspective) and directs them to improved productivity. Based on the previous research paper analysis, the researcher found that the two hypotheses were significantly positive and leads to improved productivity. They found a gendered perspective affected by workplace spirituality which leads them to improved productivity.

**Liang, Peng, Zhao and Wu (2017)** conducted study to investigate the relationship between workplace spirituality, sense of meaning in life and psychological well-being of teachers in Taiwan. The primary data were collected of 610 respondent teachers with the help of study questionnaire. The collected data were analysed using hierarchal regression to comprehend the explanatory powers of independent variables (workplace spirituality and sense of meaning in life) on the dependent variable i.e., psychological well-being. The explanatory power was recorded 62.70%. Research findings suggest that teachers should comprehend and pursue workplace spirituality to become psychologically sound and have sense of meaning in life. The author directed the future researchers to explore the predictors that effect teachers' psychological well-being.

**Khatri and Gupta (2017)** attempted to examine the potential impact of workplace spirituality on employee well-being in the organisation. The primary data were collected from 298 respondents employed in the IT, ITES and BFSI organisations located in Delhi NCR. Correlations and regression analysis were used in the study and outcome revealed that workplace spirituality has a significant relation with employee wellbeing.

**Singh and Malhotra (2017)** reviewed workplace spirituality (meaningful work, sense of community, and inner life) and its connection with glass ceiling beliefs (acceptance, resignation, denial, and resilience) and subjective success (career satisfaction, job happiness, physical & psychological well-being, and work engagement). Authors attempted to present two research models for future researchers; first, examine the relation between workplace spirituality and glass ceiling beliefs; and second, find the mediating effect of glass ceiling beliefs between workplace spirituality and subjective success. At the end, authors discussed the theoretical and practical implication of proposed models.

**Kim Seng, Gun Fie, Sarwar, Hong, Mahdee and Vinayan (2017)** presented a conceptual study to investigate the effect of workplace spirituality on employee retention among Generation Y employees working in different Malaysian organisations. This study also focuses to examine the moderating role of organisational culture as a link between workplace spirituality and employee retention. Generation Y are to be considered as sample for the study. Authors expected this study will be a great help for effective management of human resource by implementing spirituality in the workplace, specifically employee retention. By creating spiritual environment, organisational commitment can be encouraged in the workplace which results in enhanced individual productivity and performance. Authors stated that incorporation of workplace spirituality has the potential to retain employees for long term in the organisation. Organisations are providing opportunities to evolve their employees as well as the organisation itself in order to search for meaning in work which changes their focus from strictly profit oriented to a profit and employee well-being oriented.

**Petchsawang and McLean (2017)** focused their research to: (i) extend the findings of Petchsawang and Duchon (2012) in assessing the relations between workplace spirituality, work engagement, and mindfulness meditation in an eastern–context, specifically Thailand; and, (ii) evaluate the workplace spirituality and work engagement in different institutions between those who offer meditation courses and those who do not. Authors chose sample from four organisations that provide meditation courses (248 out of 300) and those who do not offer such courses (315 out of 400) in Thailand. Findings revealed that the scores of workplace spirituality and work engagement were reported higher in organisations where mediation courses were being offered as compare to those who do not. In addition, mindfulness meditation was found to be significant and positive with workplace spirituality and work engagement, and workplace spirituality also has shown full mediation relation between meditation and work engagement.

**Zsolnai and Illes (2017)** discussed about the relation between spirituality and creativity in business context. Authors considered different faith traditions such as Christianity, Hinduism, and Anthroposophy) as practical cases in order to discuss the spiritual-based creative business models. The outcome revealed that in order to enhance creativity in business, spirituality and a deep sense of connectedness are found to be significant factors. Spirituality helps in creating free space and openness which leads to a better future. It develops a gap between the self and outside pressure related to business and daily routine life. Distance is an essential condition which assists in providing ethical, rational, and creative solutions in the complex situations.

**Jaichitra and Srinivasan (2017)** conducted research to investigate the relationship of spirit at work on organisational commitment, individual productivity and in-role performance. Authors collected primary data from 551 working employees in services sector located in Bangalore and Chennai. Structured equation modeling (SEM) was incorporated to analyse the collected data. Findings indicated that spirit at work was found significantly correlated with individual productivity, organisational commitment and in-role performance. Author suggested that this research is significant as it shows the relationship of spirit at work, organisational commitment and various work related outcomes.

**Biswakarma (2018)** researched to investigate the effect of workplace spirituality on employee productivity in Nepalese hospitality organisation. The primary data were collected from 150 respondent employees using convenience sampling method. The outcome revealed a positive association between workplace spirituality and employee productivity. The author suggested that employing workplace spirituality in the organisation positively affects the employee performance and their satisfaction level. Therefore, hospitality organisations are required to emphasis spirituality at workplace in order to become sustainable and profitable organisation.

**Chatterejee (2018)** conducted research to study the impact individual and team behaviour due to workplace spirituality driven practices in the way of promoting and increasing organisational performance. The author took five major variables from literature i.e., purpose of life, sense of community, openness to experience, team experience and respect for others. The author stated, based on the literature review, that these variables have a major role in shaping individual behaviour towards designated work, colleagues and goal orientation. Survey data of 101 employees working in IT industry were collected. The findings predicted that all the variables (i.e., purpose of life, sense of community, openness to experience, respect for others and team spirit) are found important part of individual thinking and have a significant impact on the employees. All the variables were mutually reinforcing. The author found that the variables have a reasonable degree of correlation. Hence, the organisations can reinforce the workplace spirituality practices to promote individual participation in order to increase organisational performance. Enforcement of workplace spirituality within the organisation can be found more fruitful for the organisations. It promotes optimistic work attitudes among the employees which, in turn, reinforce other related work attitudes like job satisfaction, organisational commitment and employee engagement. Thus, identifying and promoting spiritual values and reinforcing them through designing work practices in the way of building sustainable organisations.

**Tayebiniya and Khorasgani (2018)** conducted research to examine the influence of workplace spirituality on job performance among the staffs of Isfahan Azad Islamic University, Iran. The study population was all the staffs employed in Isfahan Azad Islamic University i.e., 375 out of which 189 was determined as sample using Cochran method. Authors used instruments of Ashmos& Duchon(2000)'s 22-item questionnaire for workplace spirituality and Paterson (1970)'s 15-item questionnaire for job performance. Cronbach's Alpha was computed as 0.88 and 0.83 for workplace spirituality and job performance, respectively. Multi-regression analysis, Pierson correlation coefficient, and variance analytical tests were carried out using SPSS software. Results indicated that there is a significant and positive influence of workplace spirituality (r=0.330), individual's alignment with organisational values (r=0.326), a sense of connection and positive social relations with coworkers (r=0.298), meaningful work (r=0.287) and job performance. Based on the results, meaningful work was found as the best predictor of job performance.

**Saralita and Ardiyanti (2020)** presented a conference paper which aimed to investigate the effect of workplace spirituality, perceived organisational support, and organisational commitment on turnover intentions of employees working in private hospital located in Jakarta. The study also tested the relations of workplace spirituality and perceived organisational support with organisational commitment. Mediating effect of organisational commitment was also examined in the relationship of workplace spirituality and perceived organisational support with turnover intention of employees. Primary data were collected from 235 employees working in private hospital situated in Jakarta. Structural equation modeling was applied to analyse the collected data. The results indicated that workplace spirituality and perceived organisational support positively and significantly influenced organisational commitment, while organisational commitment and workplace spirituality was negatively related with turnover intention. Furthermore, organisational commitment mediated in the relationship between workplace and turnover intention. However, there is no significant relation found between perceived organisational support and turnover intention, and there is no mediation effect of organisational commitment in the relation between perceived organisational support and turnover intention.

**Hassan, Tnay, Yososudarmo and Sabil (2020)** attempted to investigate the relationship between workplace spirituality and work-to-family enrichment. This study considered three dimensions of workplace spirituality, namely, meaningful work, inner life, and sense of community. Data collection was done through survey method using questionnaire distributed to 100 respondent employees, out of which 81% responses were received, working in the two public organisations located in Kuching, Malaysia. The findings indicated that workplace spirituality (meaningful work, inner life, and sense of community) was found to have positive and significant correlation with work-to-family enrichment. It was believed that a significant effect of sense of community on work-to-family enrichment was caused by the collectivist culture of Malaysians. Therefore, the organisations are required to consider the sense of community aspect to improve work-to-family enrichment among employees, specifically religious and collectivist society context.

**Shrivastava (2020)** conducted a comparative study between spiritual and non-spiritual practices on how it affects individuals' stress level. Author considered spiritual practices (such as yoga and meditation, self-control &

tolerance, reading spiritual books, positive thinking and optimism, other spiritual practices like prayer etc.) and non-spiritual practices (eating/nutrition, entertainment like music, TV, movies etc., relaxation activities like sleeping, singing, dancing, outing, walking, outing etc., surfing internet and social media). The sample size for the study was 400 respondent faculties working in different autonomous colleges including private and public institutions of Madhya Pradesh, India. Only general colleges were considered for the study by excluding engineering and professional institutions. Simple random sampling was used for collecting the data with the help of structured questionnaire. The study found there is no significant difference found between spiritual practices and non-spiritual practices used by academic faculties.

**Rajput, Sharma and Jyotsna (2020)** conducted study to examine the effect of workplace spirituality on organisational commitment of academic staffs of general society and private establishments located in Delhi (NCR). A sample of 230 professors were finalised to participate in the study using Petchsawand and Duchon (2008)'s questionnaire of workplace spirituality and Allen and Meyer (1990)'s questionnaire of organisational commitment. In this study, workplace spirituality was a free factor, whereas organisational commitment was performed as dependent one. Using SPSS for analysing the collected, authors found there is positive and significant contribution of workplace spirituality towards organisational commitment of professors.

**Varghese and Joseph (2020)** attempted to carry out research to examine the impact of job commitment, job boredom, and work engagement on workplace spirituality of employees working in different private organisations located in different parts of India. The primary data were collected from 399 employees having 1 year of experience in private organisation of India. Descriptive statistics, regression and correlation analysis, and one-way ANOVA were applied to the collected data. The outcome revealed that job commitment found to be one of best possible organisational outcome influenced by workplace spirituality. However, work engagement was also found to be significant with workplace spirituality.

**Bharadwaj and Jamal (2020)** carried out empirical research to investigate the connection between workplace spirituality and employee performance among the I. T. professional of India. Mediating effect was also aimed to examine in the relationship between workplace spirituality and employee performance. A sample of 312 professionals working in different I. T. companies of India was taken. Applying structural equation modeling and process macro, the results showed a significant and positive connection of workplace spirituality with employee performance, however, gender was found insignificant mediator in that relationship. The author concluded that the significance of changing dehumanized workplaces into spiritual-based workplaces via developing sense of community, meaning and purpose at work, inner life, and spiritual values among employees leads them to become more performing and productive asset to the organisations, irrespective of gender variable.

# CONCLUSION

Workplace spirituality is still in nascent stage in which several dimensions are yet to be explored. However, looking at the several studies in the edition, it explains that workplace spirituality is assuredly a very significant component of sustainable organisation. We studied several effects of workplace spirituality on leadership, stress, individual performance, and organisational productivity in which it evidenced to be an extraordinary construct in the organisational setting.

# Glossary

# Bibliography


- Abdullah, A. G. K., Ismail, A. and Mydin, A. (2013). The Moderating Effects of School Principals' Leadership Practices on the Workplace Spirituality and Leadership Effectiveness Relationship.International Journal for Cross-Disciplinary Subjects in Education, 4(4): 1318-1323.

- Adnan, N., Bhatti, O. K. and Farooq, W. (2020), Relating ethical leadership with work engagement: How workplace spirituality mediates? Cogent Business & Management, 7(1): 1-22.

- Agarwal, S., & Lenka, U. (2015).Study on Work-Life Balance of Women Entrepreneurs – Review and Research Agenda. *Industrial and Commercial Training, 47*(7), 356 – 362.

- Agbim, K. C., & Oriarewo, G. O. (2012). Spirituality as Correlate of Entrepreneurship Development. *JORIND, 10*(3), 154-164.

- Ahangaran, J., Khooshebast, F. and Vahedi, E. (2016), Meta-Analysis of the effects of spirituality in the organisation and comprehensive model.

- International Journal of Advanced and Applied Sciences, 3(1): 22-31.

- Ahmed, A., Arshad, M. A., Mahmood, A. and Akhtar, S. (2016), Holistic Human Resource Development: Balancing the Equation through the Inclusion of Spiritual Quotient. Journal of Human Values, 22(3): 1-14.

- Alas, R., & Mousa, M. (2016). Organisational Culture and Workplace Spirituality. *International Journal of Emerging Research in Management & Technology*, 5(3),1-9.

- Ali, Z. and Zaky, M. (2018), Spiritual Values and Spiritual Practices: Interactive Effects on Leadership Effectiveness. Etikonomi: Jurnal Ekonomi, 17 (1): 123 – 134.

- Ashar, H. and Maher, M. (2004), Success and spirituality in the new business paradigm. Journal of Management Inquiry, 13(4): 249-260.

- Ashmos, D. and Duchon, D. (2000), Spirituality at work: conceptualization and measure. Journal of Management Inquiry, 9(2): 134-145.

- Badrinarayan, S. P. (2008), Two approaches to workplace spirituality facilitation: a comparison and implications. Leadership & Organization Development Journal, 29(6): 544-567.

- Barney, J., Wicks, J., Scharmer, C. and Pavlovich, K. (2015), Exploring transcendental leadership: a

- conversation. Journal of Management, Spirituality & Religion, 12(4): 1-15.

- Beazley, H. (1998), Meaning and measurement of spirituality in organizational settings: Development of a spirituality assessment scale. 4718-4718.

- Bell, A., Rajendran, D., & Theiler, S. (2012). Spirituality at Work: An Employee Stress Intervention for Academics. *International Journal of Business and Social Science, 3*(11), 68-72.

- Bella, R., Quelhas, O., Ferraz, F. and Bezerra, M. (2018), Workplace Spirituality: Sustainable Work Experience from a Human Factors Perspective. Sustainability, 10(2018): 1-13.

- Bharadwaj, S., & Jamal, T. (2020).In Search Of Spiritual Workplaces: An Empirical Evidence Of Workplace Spirituality And Employee Performance In The Indian I.T Industry. *International Journal of Scientific & Technology Research (IJSTR), 9*(3), 1116-1124.

- Bhunia, A., & Das, A. (2012). Explore the Impact of Workplace Spirituality on Motivations for Earnings Management-An Empirical Analysis. *International Journal of Scientific and Research Publications, 2*(2), 1-5.

- Biswakarma, G. (2018). Impact of Workplace Spirituality on Employee Productivity in Nepalese

Hospitality Organisations. *Journal of Tourism and Hospitality Education, 8*(2018), 62-76.

- Brown, R. B. ed., (2003), Organizational Spirituality – the Skeptics Version. Organization, 10, 393-400.

- Burack, E. H. (1999). Spirituality in the Workplace. *Journal of Organisational Change Management, 12*(4), 280-291.

- Cash, K. C. and Gray, G. R. (2010), A framework for accommodating religion and spirituality in the workplace. Academy of the Management Executive, 14(3): 124-134.

- Charoenarpornwattana, P. (2016). Workplace Spirituality and Human Resource Practices in Thailand. *HRD Journal, 7*(1), 82-91.

- Chatterejee, A. (2018). A Study on Workplace Spirituality Driven Practices and Its Impact on the Organization. *IOSR Journal of Business and Management (IOSR-JBM),20*(3),41-49.

- Chinomona, E. (2017). Modelling the Influence of Workplace Spirituality, Quality of Work Life, Expectations towards Work on Commitment to Long-Term Career of Employees in Gauteng Province, South Africa. *The Journal of Applied Business Research, 33*(4), 693-704.

- Crossan, M., Vera, D. and Nanjad, L. (2008), Transcendent Leadership: Strategic Leadership in

Dynamic Environments. The Leadership Quarterly, 19, 569-581.

- Davis, J. C. (2014), Self-Transcendence and Servant Leadership Behavior in New Thought Spiritual Centers: A Correlational Study. Ph.D. Thesis, University of Phoenix, 1-173.

- Dent, E. B., Higgins, M. E. and Wharff, D. M. (2005), Spirituality and leadership: An empirical review of definitions, distinctions, and embedded assumptions. The Leadership Quarterly, 16(2005): 625-653.

- Edwards, J., Van Laar, D., Easton, S. and Kinman, G. (2009), The Work-related Quality of Life Scale for Higher Education Employees. Quality in Higher Education, 15(3): 207-219.

- Fernando, M. and Jackson, B. (2006), The influence of religion-based workplace spirituality on business leaders' decision-making: An inter-faith study. Journal of management & organization, 12(1): 23-39.

- Fernando, M. and Nilakant, V. (2008), The place of self-actualization in workplace spirituality: Evidence from Sri Lanka, Culture and Religion. Journal Service science & management, 9(3): 233-249.

- Fernando, M., Beale, F. and Geroy, D. G. (2009), The spiritual dimension in leadership at Dilmah

- Tea. Leadership & Organization Development Journal, 30(6): 522-539.

- Fornaciari, C. J., Sherlock, J. J., Ritchie, W. J. and Dean, K. L. (2005), Scale Development Practices in the Measurement of Spirituality. The International Journal of Organisational Analysis, 13(1): 28-49.

- Freeman, G. T. (2011), Spirituality and Servant Leadership: A Conceptual Model and Research Proposal. Emerging Leadership Journeys, 4(1): 120-140.

- Freshman, B. (1999), An exploratory analysis of definitions and applications of spirituality in the workplace. Journal of organizational change management.12(4): 318-325.

- Fry, L. W. (2003), Toward a theory of spiritual leadership. The leadership quarterly, 14(6): 693-727.

- Gibson, A. R. (2011), Spirituality in Principal Leadership and its Influence on Teachers and Teaching.Ph.D Thesis, The University of Waikato.

- Griffiths, A. (2010), Coaching and Spiritual Values in the Workplace: exploring the perspective of coaches. International Journal of Evidence-based Coaching and Mentoring, 4(1): 65-81.

- Gull, G. A. and Doh, J. (2004), The transmutation of the Organization: Towards a More Spiritual

Workplace. Journal of Management Inquiry, 13(2): 128-139.

- Hassan, Z., Tnay, J. S., Yososudarmo, S. M. S., & Sabil, S. (2020). The Relationship Between Workplace Spirituality and Work-to-Family Enrichment in Selected Public Sector Organisations in Malaysia. *Journal of Religion and Health*,pp. 1-19.

- Heydari, Z., Soltani, H., Hojati, Z., & Heydari, O. (2013). The Relationship between Spirituality at Work and Organizational Commitment at Sports and Youth Offices of Tripartite Khorasan Provinces in Iran. *Advances in Environmental Biology, 7(14), 4848- 4853.*

- Hicks, D. ed., (2003), Religion and the Workplace: Pluralism, Spirituality, Leadership, Cambridge University Press, Cambridge, UK.

- Jaichitra, D., & Srinivasan, P. T. (2017). Spirit At Work and Its Relationship with Organisational Commitment, Individual Productivity and In-Role Performance. *Journal of Advanced Research in Dynamical & Control Systems,* 7(Spe. Iss.), 85-89.

- Jain, P. (2016), A Model for Workplace Spirituality. Advances in Economics and Business Management, 3(7): 761-764.

- Jena, L. K., & Pradhan, R. K. (2014). Workplace Spirituality and Work-life Balance: An empirical introspection in Indian Manufacturing Industries.

* *The International journal of applied philosophy*, 4(4), 155-161.

* Joseph, M. (2002), Leaders and Spirituality-A Case Study Doctoral dissertation,Ph.D thesis, University of Surrey.

* Kasinathan, S. and Rajee, M. (2019), An Empirical study on Factors of Workplace Spirituality and Organisational Outcomes. National Conference at Tuticorin, 1-8.

* Khasawneh, S., Alrjoub, S. and Zawahreh, A. (2010), Exploratory and Confirmatory Factor Analyses of the Spirituality in the Workplace Questionnaire (SWQ): A Tool for Workforce Development. Journal of Institutional Research South East Asia, 8(1): 70-85.

* Khatri, P., & Gupta, P. (2017). Workplace Spirituality: A Predictor of Employee Wellbeing. *Asian Journal of Management, 8*(2), 284-292.

* Kim Seng, V. O., Gun Fie, D. Y., Sarwar, A., Hong, L. J., Mahdee, J., & Vinayan, G. (2017). Workplace Spirituality in Enhancing Organisation Commitment that Leads to Improvement in Employee Retention of Generation Y. *Vision 2020: Sustainable Economic Development, Innovation Management, and Global Growth*,4701-11.

* Kinjerski, V. and Skrypnek, B. J. (2006), Measuring the Intangible: Development of The

- Spirit at Work Scale. In Academy of management proceedings 1, 1-6.

- Kinjerski, V. M. and Skrypnek, B. J. (2004), Defining spirit at work: Finding common ground. Journal of Organizational Change Management, 17(1): 26-42.

- Krishnakumar, S. and Neck, C. P. (2002), The "what", "why" and "how" of spirituality in the workplace. Journal of managerial psychology.17(3): 153-164.

- Kumar, R. (2017),Spiritual Leadership and Its Impact on Organizational Performance. Journal of Commerce and Trade, Society for Advanced Management Studies, 12(2): 98-105.

- Liang, J., Peng, L., Zhao, S., & Wu, H. (2017). Relationship among Workplace Spirituality, Meaning in Life, and Psychological Well-Being of Teachers. *Universal Journal of Educational Research*, *5*(6), 1008-1013.

- Lips-Wiersma, M. and Wright, S. (2012), Measuring the Meaning of Meaningful Work: Development and Validation of the Comprehensive Meaningful Work Scale (CMWS). Group and Organisation Management, 37(5): 655-685.

- Liu, C. H. and Robertson, P. J. (2011), Spirituality in the workplace: Theory and measurement. Journal of management inquiry, 20(1): 35-50.

- Lynn Stallworth, H. (2003). Mentoring, organizational commitment and intentions to leave public accounting. *Managerial Auditing Journal, Vol. 18*,No. 5, pp. 405-418.

- Marques, J., Dhiman, S. and King, R. (2005), Spirituality in the Workplace: Developing an Integral Model and a Comprehensive Definition. Journal of American Academy of Business, 7 (1): 81-91.

- Marschke, E., Preziosi, R., & Harrington, W. (2009). Professionals And Executives Support A Relationship Between Organizational Commitment And Spirituality in the Workplace. *Journal of Business & Economics Research (JBER), 7*(8), 33-48.

- Mat, N., Romli, R., Mat, N. & Noor, N. (2012). Modelling Workplace Spirituality and Teaching Effectiveness for Academician in Malaysia. *International Journal of Business and Management Studies, 4*(1), 157-164.

- McGhee, P. and Grant, P. (2008). Spirituality and Ethical Behaviour in the Workplace: Wishful Thinking or Authentic Reality. *Electronic Journal of Business Ethics and Organization Studies, Vol. 13*,No. 2, pp.61-69.

- McLaughlin, C. (1998). Spirituality at Work. *The Bridging Tree, 1*,March, 17, p.11.

- Meng, Y. (2016), Spiritual leadership at the workplace: Perspectives and theories (Review). Biomedical Reports, 5(4): 408-412.

- Mousa, M., & Alas, R. (2016). Workplace spirituality and organizational commitment :A study on the public schools teachers in Menoufia (Egypt). *African Journal of Business Management, 10*(10), 247-255.

- Muhdar, H. M. and Rahma, S. (2015), The Influence of Spiritual Intelligence, Leadership, and Organizational Culture on Organizational Citizenship Behavior: A Study to Islamic Bank in Makassar City. Al-Ulum, 15(1): 135–156.

- Nasina, M., & Doris, K. (2011). The workplace spirituality and affective commitment among auditors in big four public accounting firms: Does it matter? *Journal of GlobalManagement, 2*(2), 216 – 226.

- Neal, J. (2018), Overview of workplace spirituality research. The Palgrave Handbook of Workplace Spirituality and Fulfillment. Switzerland Cham: Palgrave Macmillan, 3-57.

- Nijhof, W. J., De Jong, M. J., & Beukhof, G. (1998). Employee Commitment in Changing

Organization: an Exploration. *Journal of European Industrial Training, 22*(6), pp. 243-248.

- Pandey, A. (2017), Workplace Spirituality: Themes, Impact and Research Directions. South Asian Journal of Human Resource Management, 4(2): 1-6.

- Pardasani, R., Sharma, R. R. and Bindlish, P. (2014), Facilitating workplace spirituality: lessons from Indian spiritual traditions. Journal of Management Development, 33, (8/9): 847-859.

- Paul, M., Dutta, A., & Saha, P. (2015). Workplace Spirituality and Work-Life Balance: A Study among Women Executives of IT Sector Companies. *International Journal of Management & Behavioural Sciences(IJMBS),6-7*, 267-277.

- Pawar, B. S. (2017), The relationship of individual spirituality and organizational spirituality with meaning and community at work: An empirical examination of the direct effects and moderating effect models. Leadership & Organization Development Journal, 38(7): 986-1003.

- Petchsawang, P. (2020), Mindfulness and Workplace Spirituality. Journal of HR Intelligence, 15(1): 118-144.

- Petchsawang, P. and Duchon, D. (2009), Measuring workplace spirituality in an Asian context. Human resource development international, 12(4): 459-468.

- Petchsawang, P., & Duchon, D. (2012). Workplace spirituality, meditation, and work performance. *Journal of Management, Spirituality & Religion, 9*(2), 189-208.

- Petchsawang, P.,& McLean, G. N. (2017). Workplace Spirituality, Mindfulness Meditation, and Work Engagement. *Journal of Management, Spirituality & Religion, 14*(3), 216-244.

- Pradhan, R., Jena, L. K. and Soto, C. M. (2017), Workplace Spirituality in Indian Organisations: Construction of Reliable and Valid Measurement Scale. Business: Theory and Practice, 18, 43–53.

- Rajput, N., Sharma, J., & Jyotsna (2020). An Empirical Study of Workplace Spirituality and Its Impact on Organisational Commitment: An Issue of Sustainability. *JAC: A Journal of Composition Theory, 13*(4), 429-447.

- Reave, L. (2005), Spiritual values and practices related to leadership effectiveness. The leadership quarterly, 16(5): 655-687.

- Rego, A., & Cunha, M. P. (2007). Workplace Spirituality and Organizational Commitment: an empirical study. *Journal of Organizational Change Management, 21*(1), 53-75.

- Rhodes, K. (2006), Six components of a model for workplace spirituality. Graziadio Business Report, 9 (2).

- Riaz, O. (2012), Spirituality and Transformational Leadership in Education. PhD Thesis,Florida International University, Miami, Florida.

- Rocha, R. G. and Pinheiro, P. G. (2020), Organizational Spirituality: Concept and Perspectives. Journal of Business Ethics, 1-12.

- Sani, A., Wekke, I. S., Ekowati, V. M., Abbas, B., Idris, I. and Ibrahim, F. (2018), Moderation Effect of Workplace Spirituality on the Organizational Citizenship Behavior. International Journal of Applied and Business and Economic Research, 16(2): 455-462.

- Saralita, M., & Ardiyanti, N. (2020). Role of Workplace Spirituality and Perceived Organizational Support on Turnover Intention: Evidence from Private Hospital in Indonesia. In *International Conference on Economics, Business and Economic Education2019, KnE Social Sciences,*pp. 206–218.

- Scroggins, W. A. (2008).Antecedents and Outcomes of Experienced Meaningful Work: A Person-Job Fit Perspective. *Journal of Business Inquiry,*pp. 68-78.

- Sheng, C. (2012). Workplace Spirituality Scale Design – The View of Oriental Culture. *Business and Management Research, 1*(4), 46-62.

- Sheng, C. and Chen, M. (2012), Chinese Viewpoints of Workplace Spirituality. International Journal of Business and Social Science, 3(15): 195-203.

- Shrestha, A. K. (2016), Further Validation of Workplace Spirituality Scale in an Eastern Context. Journal of Business and Management Research, 1(1): pp.1-13.

- Shrivastava, A., (2020). Spiritual and non-spiritual practices for work stress coping: a comparative study among academic faculties in India. *The International Journal of Indian Psychology, 8*(1), 1055-60.

- Singh, B. S. P., & Malhotra, M. (2017). Workplace Spirituality, Glass Ceiling Beliefs and Subjective Success. *International Journal of Scientific and Research Publications, 7*(7), 863-876.

- Singh, J., & Chopra, V. G., (2016). Relationship among Workplace Spirituality, Work Engagement and Grit. IOSR *Journal of Business and Management (IOSR-JBM), 18*(11), 21-27.

- Sorakraikitikul, M., & Siengthai, S. (2014). Organisational Learning Culture and Workplace Spirituality: Is knowledge-sharing behaviour a missing link. *The Learning Organisation, 21*(3), 175-192.

- Sukanya, M. (2015), Relationship between Workplace Spirituality with Leadership Effectiveness, Psychological Well-Being and Work Outcomes.Ph.D Thesis, Pondicherry University, Puducherry, 1-227.

- Tagavi, L., & Janani, H. (2014). The Relationship between Workplace Spirituality and the Organisational Climate of Physical Education Teachers in the City of Tabriz. *Indian Journal of Fundamental and Applied Life Sciences*, 4(S3), 969-973.

- Tayebiniya, N. K., & Khorasgani, N. S. (2018). The Relationship between Workplace Spirituality and Job Performance among Staff of Azad Islamic University, Iran. *Humanities & Social Science Reviews*, *Vol 6*,No 1, pp 14-18.

- Tischler, L., Biberman, J., & Mckeage, R. (2002). Linking Emotional Intelligence, Spirituality and Workplace Performance: Definitions, models and ideas for research. *Journal of Managerial Psychology*, *17*(3), 203-218.

- Vandenberghe, C. (2011), Workplace Spirituality and Organisational Commitment: An Integrative Model. Journal of Management, 8(3): 211-232.

- Varghese, A. M., & Joseph, D. M. (2020). Impact of Commitment, Boredom and Work Engagement on Workplace Spirituality in

Organisations: With Special Reference to Private Sector. *Mukt Shabd Journal,* 9(4), 642-661.

- Vyas-Doorgapersad, S. (2017). Workplace Spirituality for Improved Productivity: A Gendered Perspective. *International Journal of Social Sciences and Humanity Studies,* 9(2), 143-156.

- Wahid, N. K. B. A. (2017), The Influence of Spiritual Leadership and Workplace spirituality on Knowledge Sharing Behavior. Thesis. University of Malaya, Kuala Lumpur, 1-257.

- Wang, M., Guo, T., Ni, Y., Shang, S. and Tang, Z. (2019), The Effect of Spiritual Leadership on Employee Effectiveness: An Intrinsic Motivation Perspective. Frontiers in Psychology, 9, 1-11.

- Wheatley, M. (1999), Leadership and new science discovering order in a Chaotic World, 2nd Edition. Berret-Koehler Publishers, San Francisco.

- Wong, P. T. P. and Psych, C. (2003), Spirituality and meaning at work. International Network on Personal Meaning, President's column.

- Zsolnai, L., & Illes, K. (2017). Spiritually inspired creativity in business. *International Journal of Social Economics, Vol. 44,*No. 2, pp.195-205.